**Already published
in the *It's Wales* series:**

More to follow!

Welsh

It's Wales

Jokes

Dilwyn Phillips

First impression: 2002
Second impression: 2003

© Copyright Dilwyn Phillips and Y Lolfa Cyf., 2002

Cover design: Ceri Jones
Cartoons: Siôn Jones
Thanks also to David Jandrel

ISBN: 0 86243 619 2

Printed on acid-free and partly recycled paper
and published and bound in Wales by:
Y Lolfa Cyf., Talybont, Ceredigion SY24 5AP
e-mail ylolfa@ylolfa.com
website ylolfa.com
phone +44 (0)1970 832 304
fax 832 782
isdn 832 813

Contents

Introduction

PEOPLE ASSOCIATE WALES with singing, rugby, slate, coal-mines, and, of course, sheep. Wales is full of characters, from the Dais and Wills of the valleys to the Iantos and Evans of the mountains, and, of course, Mari fach gets everywhere, as do Marged and Myfanwy. Without these characters, Wales could be any other place in the universe. These people are true Welsh characters. Not to be confused with the village idiot, these characters are full of wit and humour. They may appear serious, but they take pride in joking about themselves.

An Irishman will laugh and joke about the Kerry man, an Australian about the Aborigines, the Americans about the Mexicans, but a true Welshman will always joke and laugh about himself.

With so many Dais and Iantos around, the popular way of distinguishing them is by the use of nicknames like Dai the Milk, or Dai Cream Top (normally the milkman or his son), or Dai the Bread, Dai Crust, and so on. The local baker once met the Prince of Wales; he became Dai Upper Crust; and the vicar of Cwmtwrch was known as Evans Above. As for Evan, he came from such a musical family that even the sewing machine was a Singer.

The Cardi, a native of the old Cardiganshire, is renowned for his tight-fistedness, and there are several stories about the Scots travelling down to Aberystwyth to finish their apprenticeships.

During my travels and research around Wales, these are some of the stories that I have encountered, told to me by friends and colleagues, all of whom I would like to thank for their generous contributions towards this book. A few of them claim that some of these stories are true and actually happened to them; indeed, some of them happened to me, but which ones?

Dilwyn Phillips

Wales

Once upon a time, in the Kingdom of Heaven, God was missing for six days. Eventually, Archangel Michael found him, resting on the seventh day. He inquired of God, "Where have you been?"

God sighed a deep sigh of satisfaction and proudly pointed downwards through the clouds. "Look, Michael; look what I've made."

Archangel Michael looked puzzled and said, "What is it?"

"It's a planet," replied God, "and I've put life on it. I'm going to call it Earth, and it's going to be a great place of balance."

"Balance?" inquired Michael, still confused.

God explained, pointing to different parts of Earth. "For example, northern Europe will be a place of great opportunity and wealth, while southern Europe is going to be poor; the Middle East, over there, will be a hot spot; and the Antarctic, down there, will be a cold spot. Over there I've placed a continent of white people, and over there is a continent of black people," God continued, pointing to different countries. "This one will be extremely hot and arid, while this one will be very cold and covered in ice."

The Archangel, impressed by God's work, then pointed to an unusually shaped land mass and said, "What's that one?"

"Ah," said God, "that's Wales, the most glorious place on Earth. There are beautiful lakes, rivers, sunsets, beaches and rolling hills. The people from Wales are going to be modest, intelligent and humorous, and they are going to be great sportsmen, singers and poets. They will be extremely sociable, hardworking, and high-achieving, and they will be known throughout the world as diplomats and carriers of peace."

Michael gasped in wonder and admiration but then exclaimed, "What about balance? You've given them everything, a perfect land, God. You said there would be balance!"

God replied wisely, "Wait until you see the neighbours I'm giving them."

The Welsh and Sport

TWO fellows were sitting in a bar in Twickenham, in a rather intoxicated state but still able to discuss any situation (intelligently, of course). The conversation came around to where they had spent their holidays, and Dai said he'd spent his in Carmarthen.

"That's great," Wil said. "The only two things to come out of Carmarthen are whores and rugby players." Dai angrily stated that his wife was from Carmarthen.

His drinking buddy, Wil, says, "Is that so... and what position does she play?"

ENGLAND play against Wales at the Millennium Stadium. Ryan Giggs has a bit of a cold and decides to spend the night before the game in the hotel. The rest of the team go out on the town, and do some clubs after. In the changing rooms, before the game, Ryan is in tip-top form; the rest of the lads are hung over and feeling very groggy. Ryan offers to go out and start the game against England on his own, until the rest feel fit enough to join in. At half time, he comes into the dressing room to find that the lads are still under the weather. He has a cuppa and announces that he's in the lead, 1-0. The lads congratulate him, and he goes back out alone for the second half. At the end of the game, he comes in a little disappointed, saying he's let the team down. The lads ask him what the final score is.

"1-1," replies Giggs. The lads say it was a tremendous performance considering he'd played on his own, but Giggs still maintains that he's let the team down. Asked his reason for thinking so, he replies, "Well, I got sent off five minutes into the second half."

A businessman from Cardiff was away on a business trip in London, and he telephoned his wife one morning. The maid answered the phone, and, being unable to lie, she told the man that his wife was in bed with the milkman. He became upset and angry, and promised the maid the earth if she would help him get his revenge by shooting the pair. After a lot of persuading, she agreed to get a shotgun from the gun cabinet, place two cartridges in the barrels and shoot his wife and the milkman, whilst he waited on the phone. After a while he heard a bang, followed by another, followed by a splash. When the maid returned to the phone, he asked her what happened, and she replied that she shot them both and threw the bodies into the swimming pool.

"Swimming pool?" he replied. "What swimming pool... ? Sorry, wrong number."

WALES v England at Twickers. Neil Jenkins is already in London, doing a book-signing in Oxford Street. He arranges to meet the rest of the team, who are travelling from Cardiff by coach, at the ground. When Neil arrives at 1 p.m., he's told that the team's coach has broken down on the M4, and will be three hours late. The ref. comes into Wales's dressing room and says the English team is not prepared to wait, and that Neil will have to play them by himself until his team shows up. The ground is packed, and about 50 Welshmen are stuck outside without tickets. Some of the Welsh boys inside the ground, on the terraces, are shouting match details down to the boys outside. Suddenly a huge cheer goes up. One of the lads outside shouts, "What happened, then?"

"Neil's just scored!"

IANTO arrived at the Pearly Gates, carrying a heavy burden, so he decided to confess his sins.

He said, "Do you know, just before the war, I played on the wing for Wales against England. We were losing by two points with just a minute to go, and the ball came right out to me. I side-stepped their wing and ran for the line, and, as I crossed, I was tackled by their centre, and grounded the ball in touch. The crowd thought that I'd scored the winning try. The ref. didn't see it, so I jumped up into the air triumphantly. The ref. awarded that winning try to Wales. I've kept that secret to this day. I've been very dishonest."

"Well, come into heaven and make yourself comfortable, Ianto."

"But, St Peter, I don't deserve this," said Ianto.

"Sh! I'm not St Peter - he's on leave. I'm St David."

"Bloody hell," said Dai. "You haven't got a dart board here as well?"

WIL tells Evan of this fantastic prostitutes' club in Cardiff. "Go down St Mary's Street, first left, then third door on the right."

Evan is absolutely amazed, so decides to try it out. The following night, Evan sees Wil and says, "You and your prostitutes club! I went there last night - it's a parachute club."

"Oops, that's torn it," says Will, "I've booked up for a jump on Saturday."

THE Welsh Rugby Union was considering replacing its president with Mathew Stevens. Explaining this unusual move, the press release stated, "We don't just need points now, we need snookers!"

A fourball were sitting around in the locker room of the local golf club after a round, when suddenly a mobile phone, which was on the bench, rings. Ianto picks it up, and the following conversation ensues:

"Hello?"

"Cariad, it's me. Are you at the club?"

"Yes."

"Great! I'm at the sale in Aber and I just saw a beautiful mink coat. It's absolutely gorgeous! Can I buy it?"

"What's the price?"

"Reduced from £2,500 to £1,000."

"Okay, but for that price I want it with all the extras."

"Great! But before we hang up, there's something else… "

"Yes?"

"It might seem like a lot, but I was going through your bank account and… I stopped by the estate agent this morning, and saw that the house we looked at last year is for sale. Remember? The one with a pool, large garden, an acre of woods, beach-front property…"

"How much are they asking?"

"Only £250,000, cariad. A magnificent price, and I see that we can afford it, anyway."

"Well, then, go ahead and buy it, but only go £225,000. OK?"

"OK, cariad. Thanks! I'll see you later! I love you!"

"Bye."

Ianto hangs up, closes the phone flap, and yells, "Hey, does anybody know whose phone this is?"

DAI is a cabbie in Cardiff. A woman hails him to take her to Bristol as she has missed her train. He drops her off in Bristol, and is immediately approached by a Yank, wanting to go to Cardiff. As they're going across the Severn Bridge, the Yank asks Dai what was the name of the bridge they were crossing.

Dai starts: "Well, sir, this is the Severn Bridge, and it's the longest…"

"In the States we have real bridges! Why, I have one twice as big as this one in my garden, and it only took six months to build." As they're driving past Cardiff Castle, the Yank asks what the building is.

"Sir, that's Cardiff Castle. It was built in..."

"I have a tool shed in my garden that's twice as big as that, and it only took three months to build!" Just then the Yank spots the Millennium Stadium, and asks Dai what it is.

Dai says: "Dunno, mate. It wasn't there this morning!"

The Welsh and Education

ON the first day of school, about mid-morning, the Infants' school-teacher turned to the class and said, "If anyone has to go to the toilet, hold up two fingers."

A little voice from the back of the room asked, "How will that help?"

WHILST out on work experience, an agriculture student from Llysfasi said to a farmer, "Your methods are too old-fashioned. I won't be surprised if this tree will give you fewer than twenty pounds of apples."

"I won't be surprised, either," said the farmer. "This is a pear tree."

A four-year-old, attending nursery school for the first time, put his shoes on by himself. The teacher noticed that the left shoe was on the right foot. She said, "Tony bach, your shoes are on the wrong feet."

He looked up at her with a raised brow and said, "Don't kid me, Miss. I know they're my feet."

ONE day, the infants' teacher was telling the story of the three little pigs to her class. She came to the part of the story where the first pig was trying to collect the building materials for his home.

"...And so the pig went up to the man with the wheelbarrow full of straw, and said, 'Excuse me, sir, but could I please have some of your straw to build my house?'"

The teacher stopped for a while, and asked her class, "What do you think the man said?"

Little Tony Jones raised his hand and said, "I think he said, 'Bloody hell! A talking pig!'"

MR Jones, the local preacher, was talking to a Sunday School group of young children about being good and going to heaven. At the end of his talk, he asked, "Where do you want to go?"

"Heaven!" Mari fach cried out.

"And what do you have to be to get there?" asked the preacher.

"Dead!" yelled Timmy.

TOMMY bach missed school on Wednesday, so Miss Davies asked him why.

"Mamgu got burnt, Miss," he replied.

"How bad was it?" asked Miss Davies.

"Oh, they don't muck about at the crematorium," he replied.

JOHNNY bach was in the garden, filling in a hole, when Mrs Jones next door looked over the fence. Curious at what Johnny was up to, she asked him, "What are doing, Johnny?"

"My goldfish died," he replied, crying, without looking up, "and I've just buried him." Mrs Jones said, "That's a big big hole for a goldfish, isn't it, Johnny?"

Johnny shovelled down the last heap of earth and then replied, "That's because he's still inside your bloody cat!"

FINDING one of the children making faces at others on the playground, Ms Smith, the nursery teacher, stopped to gently reprove the child. Smiling sweetly, she said, "Darren, when I was a child, I was told that if I made an ugly face, it would freeze and I would stay like that."

Bobby looked up and replied, "So how come you kept doing it?"

A rather annoyed Mrs Jones, whose pupil, Gethin bach, was always mischievous, finally asked him, "How do you expect to get into heaven?"

Gethin thought it over and said, "Well, I'll just run in and out and in and out and keep slamming the door until St Peter says, 'For heaven's sake, Gethin, come in or stay out!'"

WHEN Mary went to college for the first time, her mam was rather concerned and warned her over and over again never to take any boys back to her room, as she would worry about her. At the end of the Christmas term, when Mary went home, she told her mam that she now had a boy friend in college.

"I hope that you haven't taken him back to your room, Mary. You know that I'd worry about you, bach."

"No, mam," she replied. "I always went back to his room – let his mam worry!"

NINE-year-old Gethin was asked by his mother what he had learned in Sunday school.

"Well, Mam, our teacher told us how God sent Moses behind enemy lines, on a rescue mission to lead the Israelites out of Egypt. When he got to the Red Sea, he had his engineers build a pontoon bridge, and all the people walked across safely. He used his walkie-talkie to radio headquarters and call in an air strike. They sent in bombers to blow up the bridge, and all the Israelites were saved."

"Now, Gethin, is that REALLY what your teacher taught you?" his mother asked.

"Well, no, Mam... But if I told it the way the teacher did, you'd never believe it!"

The Welsh with their Women

DAI was courting Mari fach, and asked her one day: "Mari, what would you do if you were pregnant?"

"Dai, I think I would throw myself off the Menai suspension bridge."

"Jiw, Mari fach, you always were a bloody good sport."

TWM Tomos was known for his flirting with the girls, and when a lady from the city moved into Bethesda, he immediately invited her out to show her the local attractions, such as the hills, mountains, lakes, woods and so on. Whilst walking up one of the hills to the woods, he thought to himself that the city girls would expect some sort of gift on a date, not like the locals. As he didn't have any sweets or chocolates to offer, he searched his pockets and found an apple, which he kindly offered her.

"No, thank you," was the reply, "apples are for pregnant women."

"That's all right," said Twm, "you can eat it on the way home!"

DAI and a woman he's never met before find themselves in the same sleeping carriage of a train. After the initial embarrassment, they both manage to get to sleep; the woman on the top bunk, Dai on the lower.

In the middle of the night the woman leans over and says, "I'm sorry to bother you, Dai, but I'm awfully cold, and I was wondering if you could possibly pass me another blanket."

Dai leans out and, with a glint in his eye, says, "I've got a better idea... let's pretend we're married."

"Why not," giggles the woman.

"Good," he replies. "Get your own bloody blanket."

D AI and Mari had been married for over 20 years, and when asked why he had no children, he replied, "Well, you see, I'm infertile. It's hereditary in my family!"

G OMER, a powerfully built miner, meets Myfanwy at a bar in Cardiff. After a few bevvies, they agree to go back to his place. As they are making out in the bedroom, Gomer stands up and starts to undress. After taking his shirt off, he flexes his muscular arms and says, "See that, Myf. That's 1000 pounds of dynamite!"

She begins to get excited as the man drops his trousers, strikes a bodybuilder's pose, and says, "See that body, Myf. That's 1000 pounds of dynamite!" Myfanwy, is now really getting excited. Finally, he drops his underpants, and after a quick glance, Myfanwy grabs her handbag and runs screaming to the front door. Gomer catches her before she is able to leave and asks, "Why are you in such a hurry to go, Myf bach?"

Myfanwy replies, "Jiw, Gomer, with 2000 pounds of dynamite and such a short fuse, I was afraid you were about to blow!"

A FTER a few years of married life, Meirion finds that he is unable to perform. He goes to his doctor, who tries a few medicines but nothing works. Finally the doctor says to him, "Meirion, this is all in your mind," and refers him to a psychiatrist.

After a few sessions, the shrink confesses, "I don't know how to cure you, but I know this witch doctor who may be able to help." So he sends him to the witch doctor.

The witch doctor says, "I can cure this." He throws some powder on a flame, and there is a flash with billowing blue smoke. The witch doctor says, "This is powerful healing, but you can only use it once a year! All you have to do is say

'1-2-3', and it shall rise for as long as you wish!"

Meirion then asks the witch doctor, "What happens when it's over?"

The witch doctor says, "All you, or your wife, have to say is '1-2-3-4', and it'll go down. But let me warn you now; it won't work again for another year!"

Meirion goes home, and that night he is ready to surprise Blodwen with the good news. So, he is lying in bed with her and says, '1-2-3' and suddenly he gets an erection.

Blodwen turns over and says, "What did you say '1-2-3' for?"

DAI and Mari were celebrating their 50th wedding anniversary, and decided to return to Trawscoed, where they first met. They sat in a small café in the village and were telling the waitress about their love for each other, and how they met at this very spot. Sitting next to them was Celt, one of the locals, and he smiled as the old couple spoke.

After the waitress left the table, Dai said to Mari, "Remember the first time we made love? It was up in that field across the road, when I put you against the fence. Why don't we do it again, for old times' sake?"

Mari giggled like crazy and said, "Sure, why not?"

So off they went, out the door and across to the field. Celt smiled to himself, thinking how romantic this was, and decided he'd better keep an eye on the couple, so they didn't come to any harm. Dai and Mari walked to the field and, as they approached the fence, they began to undress. Dai picked Mari up when they were naked and leaned her against the fence. Celt was watching from the bushes and was surprised at what he saw. With the vitality of youth, Mari bounced up and down excitedly, while Dai thrashed around like a wild man, then they both fell to the ground in exhaustion. Eventually, they stood up, shook themselves, and got dressed.

As they walked back towards the road, Celt stepped from his hiding spot and said, "That was the most wonderful lovemaking I have ever seen. You must have been a wild couple when you were young.

"Not really," said Dai. "When we were young, that fence wasn't electric."

Dic and Lizzie Mary, just married, were in their honeymoon suite, on their wedding night. As they were undressing for bed, Dic, who was a big burly man, tossed his pants to his bride and said, "Here, put these on."

She put them on and the waist was twice the size of her body. "I can't wear your pants," she said.

"That's right," said Dic, "and don't you ever forget it. I'm the man who wears the pants in this family."

With that, she flipped him her panties and said, "Try these on."

Dic tried them on and found he could only get them on as far as his kneecaps. "Hell," he said. "I can't get into your panties!"

Lizzy Mary replied, "That's right, and that's the way it's going to be until your damned attitude changes!"

Bari comes rushing home from work, convinced that his wife Mari is having an affair with someone. After running upstairs to the flat, he looks around, sees no-one, looks out of the window, and sees the milkman leaving the block of flats. He shouts out, "Caught you red-handed!" then scans the room, sees the fridge, lifts it up and throws it out of the window on top of the milkman.

A few seconds later, at the Pearly Gates, St Peter asks the milkman, "Why are you here?"

"I don't know," said the milkman, "I was collecting my money from the milk round, and the next thing I know, something heavy landed on my head, which I now know was a fridge."

St Peter asks Bari, "Why are you here?"

"Well," he replied, "it's a bit premature. I shouldn't really be here at all; I should have trusted Mari, but you see... well, what can I say? I'm really sorry; the strain was too much for me, and I had a fatal heart attack."

St Peter says to a third man, "Why are you here?"

"Well, you see," he said, "I was sitting down in this fridge..."

DAI walks into a bar one night. He goes up to the bar and asks for a pint.

"Certainly, sir, that'll be two pence."

"TWO PENCE!" said Dai.

The barman replied, "Yes."

So Dai looks at the menu and asks, "Could I have a nice, juicy, T-bone steak, with chips, peas, and a fried egg?"

"Certainly, Dai," replies the barman, "but all that comes to real money."

"How much money?" asks Dai.

"Ten pence," he replies.

"TEN PENCE!" queries Dai. "Where's the boss of this place?"

The barman replies, "Upstairs with my wife."

Dai says, "What's he doing with your wife?"

The barman replies, "Same as what I'm doing to his business."

EVAN and Lizzie Mary went to the hospital to have their first baby delivered. The doctor said that he'd invented a machine that would transfer a portion of the labour pain to the father. He asked if they were willing to try it out. They were both very much in favour of it. The doctor set the knob at 10%, for starters, explaining that even 10% was probably more pain than the father had ever experienced before. But as the labour progressed, Evan felt fine, so he asked the doctor to bump the machine up a notch so as to ease Lizzie Mary's burden. The doctor then adjusted the machine to 20%. The doctor checked Evan's blood pressure and pulse and was amazed at how well he was doing. At 50%, Evan was still holding up fine. Since this was obviously helping out Lizzie Mary, he encouraged the doctor to transfer all of the pain. Lizzie Mary delivered a healthy baby with virtually no pain. She and Evan were absolutely thrilled. Everything was great - until they got home and found the milkman dead on their front doorstep!

AT an art exhibition in the valleys, a couple viewed a painting of three naked, very dark-skinned men, sitting on a park bench. The men on the ends of the bench had black privates, but the man in the middle had a pink one. While the couple scratched their heads, trying to figure this out, the artist walked by.

"Can I help you with this painting?" he asked.

"Well, yes," said the fellow. "Why is it the man in the middle has pink privates?"

"Oh," said the artist. "They're coal miners, and the fellow in the middle went home for lunch."

THREE old ladies are sitting in Pontypridd Park, on a beautiful spring day, feeding the pigeons and the squirrels, when, suddenly, Ianto Fullpelt, in a long trench coat, jumps in front of them and opens his coat to reveal that he is completely naked underneath it. The three old ladies haven't seen such a thing in a very long time, and their blood pressure shoots up quickly. The first old lady, Mari, lets out a gasp and has a stroke. The second old lady, Megan, sees this, and it's too much for her – she gasps and has a stroke, too. The third old lady, Myfanwy, didn't have a stroke – she was sitting too far away and couldn't reach.

IANTO goes to Tesco's with his 8-year old son. They happen to walk by the condom display, and the little boy asks, "What are these, Daddy?"

Ianto replies, "Those are called condoms, son. They use them to have safe sex."

"Oh, I see," replied the boy. "Yes, I've heard of that in health class at school." He looks over the display and picks up a pack of 3 and asks, "Why are there 3 in this pack?"

Ianto replies, "Those are for comprehensive school boys. One for Friday, one for Saturday, and one for Sunday."

"Cool!" says the boy. He notices a 6-pack and asks, "Then who are these for?"

"Those are for college students." Ianto answers, "TWO for Friday, TWO for Saturday, and TWO for Sunday."

"WOW!" exclaimed the boy; "Then who uses THESE?" he asks, picking up a 12-pack.

With a sigh, Ianto replies, "Those are for married men. One for January, one for February, one for…"

TAFF is sitting in a bar and notices two very sexy ladies in the corner, discussing the contents of a book. He tells the bartender to send them a drink on him. They just push it off to one side. He tries again, sending them another drink. They both look his way, and push the drinks away again. He gets up and walks over to them. When he gets to the table, they look up and one of the ladies says, "Thanks for the drinks, but we don't really want to be disturbed. Sorry we didn't say anything, but we're having a serious discussion about this book about the sexual performance of different races."

The other lady says, "My friend, Marged, agrees with the section that says that the American Red Indians have the longest dicks, but I feel that the part which states that Welshmen are the best lovers and are able to love all night long is more true. By the way, who are you?"

He replies, "Tonto Jones."

JOHN is in Mari fach's apartment, in a block of flats, and suddenly there's a noise outside.

"Quick," she says, "jump out of the window! My husband's coming home."

"Do you think I'm daft?" said John. "This is the thirteenth floor!"

"This is no time to be superstitious," said Mari.

IT'S a beautiful, warm spring morning, and Aled and his wife are spending the day at Chester zoo. Marged is wearing a cute, loose-fitting, pink, spring dress, sleeveless with straps. He's wearing his normal jeans and a T-shirt. The zoo is not very busy this morning. As they walk through the ape exhibit, they pass a very large, hairy gorilla. Noticing the girl, the gorilla goes ape (no pun intended.) He jumps up on the bars, and, holding on with one hand (and two feet), he grunts and pounds his chest with his free hand. He is obviously excited at pretty little Marged in the flouncy dress, and Aled, noticing the excitement, thinks this is funny. Aled suggests that Marged tease the poor fellow some more. Aled then suggests she pucker her lips, wiggle her bottom at him, and play along.

Marged, enjoying playing this game, does so, and Mr Gorilla gets even more excited, making noises that would wake the dead. Aled then suggests that she let one of her straps fall, to show a little more skin. She does, and Mr Gorilla is about to tear the bar down.

"Now try lifting your dress up your thighs and sort of fan it at him."

This drives the gorilla absolutely crazy, and now he's doing flips. Then Aled nabs his wife by the hair, rips open the door to the cage, slings her in with the gorilla and slams the cage door shut.

"Now, tell HIM you have a headache."

EVAN, a rather confident man, walks into a bar, and takes a seat next to a very attractive young woman. He gives her a quick glance, then casually glances at his watch. The young woman notices this, and asks, "Is your date running late?"

"No", he replies, "I just bought this state-of-the-art watch, and I was just testing it."

The intrigued woman says, "A state-of-the-art watch? What's so special about it?"

"It uses alpha waves to telepathically talk to me," he explains.

"What's it telling you now?"

"Well, it says you're not wearing any panties..."

The woman giggles and replies, "Well, it must be broken,

then, because I am wearing panties."

Evan explains, "Damn thing must be an hour fast."

Dai and Mari fach had a bitter quarrel on the day of their 40th wedding anniversary.

Dai yelled, "When you die, I'm getting you a headstone that reads, 'Here Lies Mari Fach, Cold As Ever'."

"Yeah" she replied, "When you die, I'm getting you a headstone that reads, 'Here Lies Dai – Stiff At Last.'"

Dai, Ianto and Wil are talking at a bar. Dai says, "I think my wife is having an affair with the electrician. The other day, I came home and found wire cutters under our bed, and they weren't mine."

Ianto says, "I think my wife is having an affair with the plumber. The other day, I found a wrench under the bed, and it wasn't mine."

Wil says, "I think my wife is having an affair with a horse." Dai and Ianto look at him aghast. "NO, I'm serious. The other day, I came home and found a jockey under our bed."

Twm is driving up a steep, narrow mountain road. Myfanwy is driving down the same road. As they pass each other, Myfanwy leans out the window and yells, "PIG"!

Twm immediately leans out his window and replies, "BITCH!"

They each continue on their way and, as Twm rounds the next corner, he slams into a pig in the middle of the road.

Evan and Myfanwy were a middle-aged couple, who had two stunningly beautiful teenage daughters. They decided to try one last time for the son and heir they'd always wanted. After months of trying, Myfanwy eventually became pregnant and, sure enough, nine months later, she delivered a healthy baby boy. Ianto, full of the joys of spring, rushed to the nursery to see his new son. He took one look and was horrified to discover the ugliest child he had ever seen. He went to his Myfanwy and said that there was no way that he could be the father of that child.

"Look at the two beautiful daughters I fathered." Then he gave Myfanwy a stern look and asked, "Have you been cheating on me?"

Myfanwy just smiled sweetly and said, "Not this time."

JOHNNY was walking down the street when he noticed his grandfather sitting on the porch, on a sun-lounger, with nothing on from the waist down.

"Dat-cu, what are you doing?" he exclaimed. The old man looked off into the distance without answering. "Dat-cu, what are you doing sitting out here with nothing on below the waist?" he asked again.

The old man slowly looked at him and said, "Well, last week, I sat out here with no shirt on, and I got a stiff neck. This is Mam-gu's idea."

ON a country road, a speed cop pulled Ianto over and said: "Sir, do you realise your wife fell out of the car several miles back?"

Ianto replied: "Thank God for that – I thought I'd gone deaf!"

The Welsh at the Pub

MOELWYN was limping home from the pub one day, when the vicar confronted him and asked him why he was walking along with one leg in the gutter.

"Oh," he replied, "Thank God for that – I thought I was lame!"

TWO young lads from the hills outside Dolgellau walked into a pub in the town, after the exams, and asked the barman for two pints of lager. The barman asked them if they were over 18.

The one smart lad answered, "18, why, I'm 20, and my brother here is 3 months older than me!"

IWAN walks into the Red and asks for three pints. The barman sets them up and then watches Iwan go through a peculiar ritual:

"Cheers, Cheers, Cheers."

Each time he says the word he drinks a pint. Then he pays and walks out. The following week, he calls at the Red again and orders the same thing. The barman watches him go through the same ritual. Curious, he asks Iwan why.

"Well," he replies, "I have a friend in America and a friend in Australia. As we can't be together, we agreed, that each weekend, we'd go into our local pub and have a round of drinks for each other. We've been doing this for 25, years since we were 18." The following week, Iwan comes in and asks the barman for two beers. The barman, a bit taken aback, places two beers in front of Iwan, and watches him say " Cheers, Cheers!"

He asks Iwan, "So who died?"

"No-one."

"But you only ordered two drinks!"

"Yeah, well, I've given up drinking."

DAI walked into a bar and ordered a martini. Before drinking it, he removed the olive and carefully put it into a glass jar. Then he ordered another martini and did the same thing. After an hour, when he was full of martinis and the jar was full of olives, he staggered out.

"Well," said a customer, "I never saw anything as peculiar as that!"

"What's so peculiar about it?" the bartender said. "Marged, his wife, sent him out for a jar of olives."

A man rushed into a bar and ordered a double martini. The man downed it in one swallow, put a five pound note on the bar, and turned and rushed out of the bar. Evan, the bartender, picked up the fiver, folded it carefully and tucked it in his vest pocket. Just at that moment, he looked up at the boss, standing in the doorway staring at him.

Doing a bit of fast thinking, he said, "Hi, boss, did you see that fellow just now? Came in here, bought a double martini, gave me a fiver tip, and rushed out without paying."

A man leaves the bar, hoping he can get home early enough not to annoy his wife for drinking after work. He gets home and finds his boss in bed with his wife. Later, back at the bar, the guy tells the bartender the story.

"Wow, that's awful. What did you do – did you shoot him?"

"Well, I carefully snuck back out the door, and hi-tailed it back here. Shoot, you ask, they were just getting started, so I figure I got time for a couple more beers first."

DAI and Ianto walked along North Parade one morning, when Ianto spotted the landlord of the Bull cleaning the steps, so quickly he told Dai to follow him, and he proceeded into the Bull.

"Excuse me," said the landlord, "we don't open 'till 11.00 o clock, and it's only 9.30 now."

"Oh, sorry," replied Ianto, "we saw the door open and naturally thought that you were open. It's all right – we'll come back later."

As they turned to walk away, the landlord asked them if they were strangers in town, and, on establishing this and finding that they had nothing else to do, invited them in to sit down and wait until opening time, and read the local paper.

Two minutes later, he appeared behind the bar and duly said, "Would you like to buy a pint whilst waiting for me to open?"

AFTER a rather heavy session, the barman asks Evan, who's lying on the floor: "Would you like a chair there, mate?"

"No, I'm okay standing, thanks."

EVAN walks into a bar, goes up to the counter, and the barman notices a large steering wheel, with a parrot perched atop it, sticking out of Evan's flies. He says to Evan, "Hey, Evan, do you realise you have a steering wheel, with a parrot on it, sticking out of your flies?"

Evan replies, "Aye! He's driving me nuts!"

IANTO walks into a bar, sits down and says, "Give me a pint, before the problems start."

The barman doesn't understand but gives Ianto a pint.

15 minutes later, Ianto orders another beer, saying, "Give me a pint, before the problems start."

The barman looks a little bit confused, but pours Ianto a pint. This carries on the whole night, and after the 15th pint, the barman is totally confused, and asks Ianto "What do you mean by saying 'Before problems start', and when are you going to pay for your beer?"

Ianto answers, "You see, right now, the problems are starting!"

Dai goes to have a drink in his favourite local, and drinks one whisky after another, until he's so drunk that he starts mumbling to himself. His mate, the barman, asks him: "What's the matter, Dai? Got problems at home?"

"Yeah, big ones.... Myfanwy, the wife, you know, she's terrible. I can't stand her."

"But why do you say that? She's such a nice lady."

"She's terrible, I tell you. She's a pig. She's so dirty, she's disgusting."

"But why? I know that Myfanwy has a reputation as the best wife in the village! Always helping out in chapel."

"I'm telling you, she's disgusting. She leaves the dishes piling up in the kitchen sink."

"So, what's so bad about that?"

"It's disgusting, I tell you, 'cause where am I gonna pee now?"

Dai walks into his local and tells the barman, "Hey, Jerry – the usual."

Without hesitation, the barman brings Dai his favourite drink. Dai proceeds to tell the barman of how his wife has been bitching about how much time he spends there, and how she's always doing for him and never getting anything in return. So the barman suggests that Dai go home early tonight and spend some time with her. Reluctantly, Dai agrees and goes home, only to find his wife packing her suitcases. He asks her where in the hell she thinks she's going. She replies, "Rhyl. A friend tells me that they'll pay me £25 a time for my body, and I've been giving it to you for free!"

So Dai starts packing his suitcases, too. When she asks him where the hell he thinks he's going, he replies, "Rhyl. I want to see how you're going to live on £50 a year!"

ANYWAY, this fellow from the Rhondda went into a bar in Cardiff, where he found one other customer leaning against the bar.

"Can I buy you a drink, Taff?"

"That's kind of you," replied the other.

"Tell me," said the first, "where are you from?"

"From the Rhondda," replied the second.

"That's amazing! I'm from the Rhondda, too. Have another drink."

"Which school did you go to in Rhondda?" said the first.

"Tonypandy CP, on the Ponty road," said the second.

"That's amazing," said the first, "I went to Tonypandy CP on the Ponty Road, too.

Have another drink."

"When did you leave?" said the first.

"June 1966," said the second.

"That's really amazing," said the first, "I left in June 1966, too. Have another drink."

Just then another customer walked in and asked the barman what was going on.

"Oh, nothing," said the barman. "Only the Williams twins getting drunk again!"

HARRI, who has spent over four hours with his mates in the Red Lion, decides that he'd better be heading off home, if he doesn't want to be nagged by his wife. So, he says "bye," to everyone and leaves to go home. He is so drunk, that in the middle of the street, he starts shouting out loud: "I'm Jesus! I'm Jesus! I'm Jesus!"

Wil, who was on the other side of the road, looks at him and recognises Harri. So he goes towards him, takes him by the arm and tells him: "You can't say things like that - are you mad?"

Harri answers, "But I am Jesus! You don't believe me? Come with me, and I'll show you that you're wrong!"

So they both walk towards the pub he had just left and, as soon as he walks in, the barman looks at him and says, "Jesus, not you again!"

So, in the bar were Dai, Wil and Ianto.
Dai says, "My wife is so stupid, she bought £300 worth of meat, and we don't even have a freezer."

"That's nothing," says Wil, "my wife is so thick, she bought a £6,000 car, and she can't even drive!"

"Pah," says Ianto, "my wife is so stupid, she booked a to trip to Ibiza, and bought 1000 condoms, and she hasn't even got a dick!"

Gomer walks into a bar and says to the bartender, "Beer for me, beer for you, and beer for everyone who's in the bar now."

After drinking, Gomer starts walking out of the bar. "Hey, what about the payment?" yells the barman.

"I have no money," answers Gomer.

The barman hears that and gives Gomer a hiding as hard as he can, then throws him out into the street. The next evening, Gomer walks into the bar again and says to the barman, "Beer for me, beer for you, and beer for everyone who's in the bar now."

The barman thinks to himself, "The man can't be stupid enough to pull the same trick twice, tonight he must have enough money," and gives beer to everyone. After drinking, Gomer starts walking out of the bar.

"Hey, what about the payment?" yells the barman.

"I have no money," answers Gomer.

The barman hears that and gives Gomer another hiding, even worse, then throws him out into the street.

One evening later, Gomer walks again into the bar and says to the barman, "Beer for me, and beer for everyone who is now in the bar."

In disgust, the barman asks, "What, no beer for me this time?"

"No," answers Gomer, "you get violent when you drink."

DAI walks into a bar in Clydach and orders a beer. While chatting with the barman, Dai says, "I have a method that will enable you to double the amount of beer you sell every day."

"Really?" says the barman, "How?"

"Very simple. Just pour full glasses."

CEREDIG walks into a bar and orders a sweet sherry. He starts drinking his sherry, and notices a crocodile sitting at the end of the bar. He asks the barman, "What is that croc doing, sitting down there?"

The barman says, "He does tricks."

Ceredig then says, "Oh, yeah?"

The barman asks, "Do you want to see one?"

Ceredig replies, "Yes."

The barman grabs a baseball bat from behind the bar, walks down to the end of the bar, puts his privates in the croc's mouth, and whacks the croc on the side of its head! The croc doesn't move an inch. The barman walks back to Ceredig, turns to everyone in the bar, and says he'll give £25 to anyone else who does that.

Ceredig says, "OK then, but don't hit me over the head quite so hard!"

A blonde walks into a bar in Aberaeron, and the barman says the drinks are on the house. When the barman looks up, there's the blonde sitting on the roof.

He asks, "What are you doing up there?"

She replies, "You told me the drinks were on the house."

MANAGER walks into club bar. Bertie is standing at the bar drinking a pint, while a whole bunch of members are standing in the far corner, drinking. Manager asks members, "Why so unsociable? Why not join Bertie, all by himself at the bar?"

They reply, "We would like to, but there is a terrible smell there."

"What kind of smell?" asks the manager.

"You go over there and find out for yourself," they say.

Manager walks over to Bertie and, sure enough, there is a terrible smell. He says to Bertie, "I say, you smell as though you have done something in your pants!"

Bertie puts down his beer and says, "That's right, I have."

Manager says, "In deference to the other members, don't you think you should go to the bathroom and clean yourself up?"

"No, I don't think so," says Bertie. "I haven't quite finished yet!"

JONES walks in to a bar and sees Myfanwy at the other end of the bar. He walks up to her and they start to flirt and joke around. After an hour or so, they decide to go back to her place. They get there and Jones can't perform. Myfanwy asks why, and he says, "Well, my wife told me not to drink any more, and if she finds out about this, she'll kill me!"

Myfanwy says, "Relax and think of Wales. I'll take care of everything for you."

So they have a great night. Around four in the morning, Jones gets up to leave, and Myfanwy sticks a piece of chalk behind Jones's ear, and rubs some talcum powder on his hands. So, finally, Jones gets home, and his wife is waiting for him at the door. She asks him where he's been, and he says,

"Cariad, I went to the bar tonight and I was just going to have a couple of drinks and then I saw this beautiful woman, Myfanwy, and I couldn't help it... we went back to her house, and we spent the rest of the night in bed together."

The wife grabs his hands, sees the powder, and says, "You're such a liar! You've been playing darts with the boys again! You've still got the chalk behind your ears!"

HUW walks into this same bar every time he comes from work, and all the time says to the barman, "Give me a woman!"

And the barman tells him, "We don't have women around here."

So Huw leaves. Next day, Huw calls again as usual and says to the barman, "Give me a woman."

"No women around here," says the barman. So Huw leaves. The barman says, "I bet that guy will be here tomorrow again." So, what he does is, he inflates one of those blow-up dolls, and puts it upstairs. So, when Huw walks into the bar again, and says to the barman, "Give me a woman," the barman replies, "Fine, she's right upstairs, waiting for you."

"OK," said Huw. So he goes upstairs. When Huw doesn't return, the barman is eventually worried.

"Where is this guy? He's been up there for two hours. What the hell is going on?" So he goes upstairs, opens the door, and sees the guy crying on the bed. "What happened? Where's the girl?" said the bartender.

"I gave her a love bite, and she flew out the window!"

A N old Englishman walked into a bar and asked for a bottle of 38-year-old wine from Leone, France. The barman, not wanting to go to the cellar, gave the Englishman the closest bottle of wine he has.

The Englishman tasted it, and said: "This wine is only two years old, and is from Santiago de Chile." The barman was amazed, but at the same time curious, so he gave him another bottle. The Englishman goes: "This wine is 17 years old and is from San Diego, California." The barman was so amazed that he gave him another bottle. The Englishman tasted it and said: "This wine is 30 years old and is from Lima, Peru." Finally, the barman went to the cellar, got the right bottle, and gave it to the Englishman. The Englishman said: "Finally, a 38-year-old wine from Leone, France."

Dai, who had been watching, went up to the Englishman, and said: "Could you please tell me what kind of drink this is," and handed him a cup.

The old Englishman tasted it, and said: "What the hell? This is piss!"

And Dai replied: "Yeah, I know, but could you please tell me from where, because I'm so drunk that I don't remember where I live."

A LFIE, one of the regulars from this bar, is found passed out cold very late one night. The barman wakes Alfie and tells him to go home. Well, Alfie makes it home, only to find his wife, Megan, with her suitcase in the car, ready to go home to her mother. Megan tells him how she's fed up with his terrible habit, and bids him a final farewell. Alfie tries to tell her that it wasn't his fault, that this new bar he was drinking at was a private place, with everything in gold. Megan stops, and asks him to explain.

So Alfie says, "Yeah, I sat down, and the stools were made of gold; I asked for a shot of Tequila, and the glass I was served with, well, that was gold, too." He went on talking about the gold counter top and the gold walls and the gold urinals.

Megan, a tad unsure of his story, finds the bar in the local listings, calls the manager, and asks if they served drinks in gold glasses, and the manager confirmed that they did. She asked about the gold stools and the gold walls, again the manager confirms everything. Megan, feeling really bad that she didn't believe Alfie, apologises to the manager for taking up his time, telling him how her husband tried to lie to her again, about some new bar with everything fitted out in gold. Laughing out loud, she says, " Wow! I never heard of a place with gold urinals."

"Urinals?" the manager asks Megan.

"Yes, my Alfie said that even the urinals were gold."

The manager, putting her on hold, looks over to the leader of the bar's resident band, and says, "Hey, man – I think I've found that guy that pissed in your saxophone."

T WM walks into a bar, with a steak and kidney pie on his head. He walks to the barman and says, "Can I have a pint, please?" The barman gets him his pint, and stares at the pie on his head, but doesn't like to ask him about it.

But he can't stand it any longer, so he says, "Excuse me, Twm, but what's that steak and kidney pie doing on your head?"

He replies, "I always have a steak and kidney pie on my head on a Thursday."

The barman says, "But it's Wednesday today!"

So Twm says, "Oh, I must look like a right prick, then!"

AFTER a night out on the town, Dai goes to the fair in Aberystwyth. He goes to the rifle stall, and scores a bull with every shot. He is given a tortoise as first prize. The following Monday, he again visits the fair, after another night out, calls at the same stall, and again scores with every shot, then tells the attendant, "The pie I won last week was lovely, but can you give me one that's not quite so crusty this time?"

IANTO, a depressed 40-year-old who's hit mid-life crisis, walks into the Institute, just after breaking up with his wife, who's left him after 20 years. How bad do you think he felt? Having finished his fifth double whisky, he noticed two attractive young blondes sitting at the end of the bar. He was feeling quite relaxed and confident, so he gestured to the barman to lean over the bar, and whispered that he wanted to buy the two blondes a drink.

The barman said, "Don't bother, Ianto, they're both lesbians. They're regulars here."

The guy replies, "What the heck, I'll still buy them a drink," as he thought of his wife.

The barman put the drinks on the bar before the blondes, and gestures that they're from the guy at the other end of the bar. He smiled, and said, "Yes! And he still insisted."

"Well," said the blue-eyed blonde, "this guy deserves a thankyou." So they both pick up their drinks, walk over to Ianto, and both ask in unison, in their sexiest voices, "May we join you?"

Ianto quickly responds, "Why, sure, girls! Be my guests," and gestures with his hand to the stools on either side of him. Both sit down, one on either side of him, and begin a long and profound discussion.

"Tell me," said Ianto eventually. "What part of Lesbia do you come from?"

IANTO is walking into a hotel bar. As he does so, he bumps into a very attractive woman. Ianto says,

"Sorry. If your heart is as soft as your breast, I know you will forgive me."

To which the woman replies, "If your privates are as hard as your elbow, I'm in room 211."

Dafydd walks into a pub and says, "Pie and chips, please. The barman fetches the food, Dafydd sits down, eats the chips, puts the pie on his head and walks out. The barman is confused.

Next day, Dafydd returns to the pub, and orders another pie and chips. The barman serves him his meal, Dafydd eats the chips, puts the pie on his head, and walks out. The barman only just resists the temptation to ask him what he's doing.

The following day, Dafydd again returns to the pub and orders another pie and chips. The barman says, "Sorry, we're out of pies today, but you can have pastie and chips if you want." Dafydd accepts the pastie and chips, sits down and eats the chips, and then puts the pastie on his head. He's just about to walk out, when the barman collars him, and asks, "Oi, mate, why have you got that pastie on your head?"

Dafydd replies, "Well, you haven't got any pies."

DAI walks into a bar and, after a few drinks, approaches Annie, standing alone.

"Would you like to dance?"

Annie retorts, "I don't care for this song, and surely wouldn't dance with you, Dai."

Dai replies, without blinking an eye, "I'm sorry, you must have misunderstood me. I said you look fat in those trousers."

TWM walks into a bar and says, "Barman, give me a whisky." He takes the whisky, then looks in his pocket. "Bartender! Give me another whisky!" He takes the whisky, then looks in his pocket. He says, "Bartender, another whisky." He takes the whisky then looks in his pocket.

The bartender says, "Twm, why is it, that after every drink, you look in your pocket?"

"I have a picture of my wife Megan, and when she looks good, I'll go home!"

EFFRAIM is sitting at a bar just looking at his drink. He stays like that for half an hour. Then, a big, trouble-making collier steps next to him, takes the drink from Effraim, and just knocks it back. Poor Effraim starts crying.

The collier says, "Come on, Effraim. I was just joking. Let me buy you another. I just can't stand seeing a grown man cry."

"No, it's not that. Today's the worst day of my life. First, I fall asleep; I'm late to work, and I miss the cage underground. The colliery manager, in a rage, fires me. When I leave the pit and go to drive home, I find my car's been stolen. The police say they can do nothing. I get a taxi home, and when I leave it, I remember I left my wallet behind. The taxi driver just drives away. I go home and, when I get there, I find my wife sleeping with the milkman, so I leave home and come here. And when I'm just about to finish it all, you show up and drink my poison."

Gomer rushes into the Cooper's, orders four large malts, and has the landlord line them up in front of him. Then, without pausing, Gomer quickly downs each one.

"Whew," said the landlord, "you seem to be in a hurry."

"You would be, too, if you had what I have."

"What do you have?" the barman asked.

"Eighty-five pence."

The Welsh Country People

A Cardiff woman married a Ceredigion farmer and brought him to the city for the first time. When they first arrived, she got them a hotel room, and as they were lying in bed, she looked over in the corner and saw a used condom.

"Oh, yuck!" she exclaimed, pointing it out to her new husband.

He stretched over to see what it was. Then he looked at her and asked, "What is it?"

"Why, it's a disgusting, used, sheepskin condom!" she replied. "Don't they use them in Ceredigion?"

"Aye, sure," he said, "but we don't skin 'em first!"

As Pete the Meat, the local butcher, is shooing a dog from his shop, in the dog's mouth he notices £10 and a note which reads: '10 lamb chops, please.' Amazed, he takes the money, puts a bag of chops in the dog's mouth, and quickly closes the shop. He follows the dog and watches as it waits for a green light, looks both ways, and trots across the road to a bus stop. The dog checks the timetable and sits on the bench. When a bus arrives, it walks around to the front and looks at the number, then boards the bus. Pete follows, dumb-struck. As the bus travels out into the country, the dog takes in the scenery. After a while it stands on its hind legs to push the 'stop' button, then Pete follows it off. The dog runs up to a farmhouse and drops the bag on the doorstep. It then goes back down the path, takes a big run, and throws itself – whap! – against the door. The dog does this repeatedly. No answer. So it jumps on a wall, walks around the garden, bangs its head against a window, jumps off, and waits at the front door. A big farmer opens it and starts cursing and kicking the dog.

Pete runs up and screams at the farmer: "What the hell are you doing? This dog's a genius!" The farmer responds, "Genius, my arse. It's the second time this week he's forgotten his key!"

TWM Tregaron was a very, very rich and successful, internationally-known, Welsh landowner. One day, on his beautiful estate, situated just outside Tregaron, the BBC was interviewing him about his life and times, and the following occurred:

"You see," he says, "this is where it all began. This is the very land upon which I was born, and where I grew up. Over there," he points to a humble cottage, "is where I was born, where my father was born, and his father, ya da ya da, blah, blah..." He goes on: "Yes, these hills are where I grew up! Why, just over there, you see that little hill, with the gnarled old conker tree?"

"Oh, yes, How pretty. How idyllic."

"Well," he says, "just under that oak tree is where I had my first sexual experience. And you see that bush on the other little hill over to the left? That is where her mother stood and watched!"

"Oh? And what did her mother say?"

"Baaaaaa!"

DAI was in the process of selling one of his prize stallions to a rich lady from the north of England. He explained to her that the horse was well-balanced with a leg at each corner.

"What about his fetlock?" enquired the lady.

"Yes, yes," replied Dai, "very good, and he's got a pretty face, and a nice tail, too."

"Hm," said the lady, "and how far back does his pedigree go?"

"Well, I can't really tell," said Dai, "but when it's out, it touches the floor."

IANTO, Penrhiw farm, approached his bank manager with a view to getting a bank loan.

"I'm afraid, Ianto, that you're overdrawn to the hilt now,

and there's nothing being paid back in," replied Mr Thomas.

"But sir," said Ianto, "you see, I've got my eye on this brand new tractor which will help me plough the fields, and collect my sheep from the hills."

"How much?" said the bank manager.

"£40,000," replied Ianto.

"Well," said the bank manager, "just keep your eye on it, because you'll never get your arse on it!"

A farm boy from Ceredigion joined the army, and after basic training and on his first leave his father asked him what he thought of army life.

"It's pretty good, Dad. The food's not bad, the work's easy, but best of all, they let you sleep real late in the morning."

THERE was a farmer in Pembrokeshire who had many pigs. One day, a stranger visited the farm and asked him, "What do you feed to your pigs?"

"Well, I give them acorns, corn, and things like that. Why?"

"Because I'm from the Animal Welfare Association, and you're not feeding them properly. They shouldn't be fed waste material." Then he fined the farmer.

Some days later, another fellow arrived, and asked the same question. The farmer answered: "Well, I feed them very well. I give them salmon, caviar, shrimp, steak... why?"

"Because I'm from the United Nations, and it's unfair that you feed your pigs like that when there are people starving to death." And he fined the farmer.

Finally, another man came, and asked the same question. The hesitant farmer answered after a few minutes: "Well, I give each pig a fiver so they can buy whatever they want."

TWO cows were talking in the field one day.
First Cow: "Have you heard about the mad cow disease that's going around?"

Second Cow: "Yeah, makes you glad you're a penguin, doesn't it?"

THERE was a farmer in Abergynolwyn, who had several fields of peas. His biggest problem was the local kids, who would constantly pinch some every single night. After some careful thought, he came up with a clever idea, that he thought would scare the kids away for sure. So, he made up a sign, and posted it in the field. The next day, the kids showed up and saw this sign, which said, "Warning!! One of the peas in this field has been injected with cyanide."

So the kids ran off, made up their own sign and posted it next to the sign that the farmer had made. The farmer showed up the next week and, when he looked over the field, he noticed that the peas were intact, and none were missing, but he noticed a new sign next to his. He drove up to the sign which read: "Now there are two."

A retired ventriloquist moved to Tregaron and went into the local for a bevvie. Seeing a parrot in its cage on the bar, he decided to have some fun, so he turned to the parrot and asked him what life was like in the pub, to which the parrot replied,

"Life? This is no life! They place me here on top of the bar and expect me to copy some silly phrases like 'pretty polly.' Life? It's really boring here."

With that, he turned to the cat and asked him how he felt. The cat complained that the locals were really inconsiderate people, stepping on him, spilling beer and so on. By now the whole village had heard about this fellow who could talk to the animals, and the bar quickly filled up.

He then proceeded to ask the dog his views, to which the dog replied that everyone expected him to retrieve beer-mats when all he wanted to do was rest, and locals breathed cigarette smoke over him, which affected his barking, and so on.

At this point, the landlord rushed out of the bar, out of the building and into the barn. He promptly turned to the sheep and said,

"Listen, mate, if anyone comes in here asking you any questions, just keep your bloody mouth shut – right?"

Q. What do you call a sheep without any legs in Bethania?

A. A cloud.

TWO sheep in a field, and one says "Baaaaaa.."
"You spiteful thing," said the other, "I was just going to say that."

WHAT three lies does a Nebo YFC member tell?
  1. I own my own farm.
  2. I do have a pickup truck.
  3. Honestly, I was only trying to help that sheep over the fence!

HOW do Powys sheep herders practice safe sex? By marking the sheep that kick with a big X!

A tourist was driving through a small town in Ceredigion and passed a restaurant. He wanted to make a U-turn, but saw a policeman just up ahead. He pulled up and asked the officer,

"Excuse me, but can you make a U-turn?"

The officer looks at the fella and says, "Well, hell, yeah! I can even make her eyes bulge!"

Q. What do you call a guy standing on a corner in Wales, with a sheep under each arm?

A. A pimp.

A young man moves to a village in Wales and gets talking to an old man from the village. He asks the old man what his name is. The old man gets very irate at this point and says,

"See that line of houses over there? I built them all, but do they call me Jones the Builder? Do they hell! See those railway lines over there? I laid them all, but do they call me Jones the Engineer? Do they hell! See those bridges over that river? I built them all, but do they call me Jones the Bridge Builder? Do they hell! But, a long, long time ago, I made love to one sheep..."

A sheep farmer needs to get his sheep pregnant for next year's lambing season. However, his male ram has died and he, unfortunately, has no money to buy a new one. He decides to phone a business advisor for some help, and explains his situation. The business advisor says that the farmer will have to get the sheep pregnant by his own natural means. The farmer agrees to this, having no other options. So he gets all the sheep into the farm lorry and takes them to a quiet wood nearby to do the business. On his return to the farm, he contacts his business advisor and asks how will he know if the sheep are pregnant. The business advisor tells him that if the sheep are pregnant, they will act strange and funny, lying on their backs and kicking their legs in the air.

The farmer goes to bed and, next morning, looks out of his

window to see if the sheep are acting strange and funny, lying on their backs, kicking their legs in the air. But they are not acting strange nor funny, lying on their backs, nor kicking their legs in the air. He phones his business advisor and tells him the situation. The business advisor tells the farmer that they are not pregnant, and he will need to do the business to the sheep again. The farmer has no option but to agree; he gets all the sheep back into the farm lorry and takes them back to the quiet woods and again does the business. He returns to the farm and goes straight to bed, telling his wife not to wake him up in the morning due to the fact that he's knackered.

Morning duly comes, and the farmer's wife comes running into the bedroom, she wakes up her husband and tells him that the sheep are acting strange and funny.

The farmer jumps up and says, "Are they lying on their backs kicking their legs in the air?"

To which the wife says, "No, they're all in the lorry, beeping the horn."

GARETH is sitting in the Red, getting drunk. Sion comes in and asks Gareth,

"Hey, why are you sitting here, on this beautiful day, getting drunk?"

Gareth replies, "Some things you just can't explain."

Sion: "So what happened that's so horrible?"

Gareth: "Well, today I was milking the cow. Just as I got the bucket about full, she kicked the bucket with her left leg."

Sion: "OK, but that's not so bad."

Gareth: "Some things you just can't explain."

Sion: "So, what happened then?"

Gareth: I took her left leg and tied it to the post on the left.

Sion: "And then?"

Gareth: "Well, I sat back down and continued to milk her. Just as I got the bucket about full, she kicked the bucket with her right leg."

Sion: "Again?"

Gareth: "Some things you just can't explain."

Sion: "So, what did you do then?"

Gareth: "I took her right leg this time and tied it to the post on the right."

Sion: "And then?"

Gareth: "Well, I sat back down and began milking her again. Just as I got the bucket about full, the stupid cow knocked over the bucket with her tail."

Sion: "Hm."

Gareth: "Some things you just can't explain."

Sion: "So, what did you do?"

Gareth: "Well, I didn't have any more rope, so I took off my belt and tied her tail to the rafter. That moment, my pants fell down and my wife walked in... Some things you just can't explain."

THE new congregational minister was arriving at Tregaron. One of the members met him at the train, with his horse and trap, to drive him to his new chapel. As they were going along the way, they passed a man in a pasture, having his wicked way with a cow. The preacher was horrified; his chauffeur, however, seemed completely undisturbed, and continued driving. Soon they passed another field, where the preacher witnessed a man having his wicked way with a sheep. Again, there was no reaction from his chauffeur. A little further down the road, they came upon a man, standing out in his field playing with himself. The preacher couldn't take any more.

"Stop right here, right now," he told his chauffeur. The

preacher got out and went over to the field. "I don't get it," he said. "First we pass a man having his way with a cow, then we pass a man having his way with a sheep, and now we come upon you and you're playing with yourself. Can you tell me what is going on here?"

"Well, Minister," the man drawled, "many of us out here are poor folk, so not everybody can afford an animal."

M RS Jones's bull sadly passed away. Sometime later, the cow needed servicing, so she phoned up Davies Tan-y-Bwlch, asked him if he'd bring his bull over to the cow, and was informed that his bull had also passed on to greener pastures.

"Oh! What shall I do now," she said, "with no bull for my Daisy?"

Mr Davies replied that Evans the Vet could service her cow with his Artificial Insemination.

She rang Evans the Vet, and explained her problem. He promised to come over in the morning, saying that would need a bowl of hot water with which to clean himself afterwards. The following morning, Evans turned up as promised.

Mrs Jones greeted him and told him, "I've got the bowl of hot water in the cow-shed ready for you, and a towel. I've also knocked a nail in the barn door, for you to hang your trousers up!"

A big-city solicitor was representing Railtrack in a case filed by a mid-Wales farmer. Farmer Cledwyn's prize bull was missing from the section through which the railway passed. The farmer only wanted to be paid the market value of the bull. The case was scheduled to be tried before the magistrates. The Railtrack solicitor immediately cornered Farmer Cledwyn, and tried to get him to settle out of court. The solicitor did his best selling job, and finally Farmer Cledwyn agreed to take half of what he was asking.

After Farmer Cled had signed the release and taken the cheque, the young solicitor couldn't resist gloating a little over his success, telling him, "You know, I hate to tell you this, old man, but I put one over on you in there. I couldn't have won the case. The train driver was asleep and the guard was in the toilet when the train passed your farm that morning. There wasn't a single witness to put in the dock. I bluffed you!"

Farmer Cled replied, "Well, I'll tell you, young feller, I was a little worried about winning that case myself, because that bloody bull came home this morning."

OLD Jones, the farmer, and his wife, Megan, were leaning against the edge of their pig-pen when Megan recalled that the next week would mark their golden wedding anniversary.

"Let's have a party, Ianto," she suggested. "Let's kill a pig."

Ianto scratched his grizzled head. "Megan," he answered, "I don't see why the pig should be blamed for something that happened fifty years ago."

YOUNG Dai, Farmer Jones's son, was returning to Tregaron from the market, with the crate of chickens his old man had entrusted to him, when, all of a sudden, the box fell and broke open. Chickens fled in different directions, but young Dai tramped all over town, scooping up the wayward birds and returning them to the repaired crate. Hoping he had found them all, Dai reluctantly returned home, expecting the worst.

"Hey, Dad," he confessed, "the chickens broke loose, but I managed to find all twelve of them."

"Well, that's not bad, Dai," his father replied. "You only had seven to start with."

The Welsh and Religion

MYFANWY goes to church to confess her sins to the priest. "Forgive me Father, for I have sinned."

"Tell all of your sins, Myfanwy."

"Oh, Father, last night my Ianto made hot, passionate love to me seven times," she says.

The priest thinks about this long and hard and says, "Take seven lemons, squeeze the juice into a tall glass, and drink it."

"Will this cleanse my soul of my sins?"

"No," the priest says, "but it'll wipe that bloody smile off your face!"

BESSIE went to the Methodist preacher with a problem. "Mr Jones, sorry to trouble you, but I have two female parrots, and they only know how to say one thing. All they ever say is, 'Hi, we're prostitutes, and we want some fun.' It's embarrassing when visitors come to the house; what should we do about it?"

"That's terrible!" replied Mr Jones, "but I think I can help. Bring your two female parrots over to my house, and I'll put them with my two male parrots that I taught to pray and read the Bible. My parrots will teach your parrots to stop saying that terrible phrase, and they'll learn to praise and worship."

Next day, Bessie brought her female parrots to Mr Jones's house. His two male parrots were holding their bibles and quietly praying in their cage. Bessie put her two female parrots in the cage with the male parrots. The females said, "Hi, we're prostitutes, and we want to have some fun."

One of the minister's parrots looked at the other, and exclaimed, "Put your bible away – our prayers have been answered!"

MOELFRYN, a poor farmer from Pen-y-groes, was brought to Mercy Hospital, for coronary surgery. The operation went well, and as he regained consciousness, he was reassured by a Sister of Mercy waiting by his bed.

"Moelfryn, you're going to be just fine," the nun said, while patting his hand. "We do have to know, however, how you intend to pay for your stay here. Are you covered by insurance?"

"No, I'm not," Moelfryn whispered hoarsely.

"Can you pay in cash?"

"I'm afraid I can't, Sister."

"Do you have any close relatives, then?"

"Just my sister who works in New Mexico," Moelfryn replied, "but she's a spinster nun."

"Nuns are not spinsters, Moelfryn," the nun replied. "They are married to God."

"Okay," Moelfryn said with a smile. "Just send the bill to my brother-in-law."

EDRYD lived alone, in the mountainside above Upper Chapel, with only a pet corgi, Pero, for company. One day, Pero died, and Edryd went to the Baptist Minister and asked,

"Preacher, my dog is dead. Could you say a prayer for the poor creature in chapel next Sunday?"

The preacher replied, "I'm afraid not; we cannot have services for an animal in the chapel, but there is a new denomination down the lane, and there's no telling what they believe. Maybe they'll do something for Pero."

Edryd said, "I'll go right away preacher. Do you think £500 is enough to donate for the service?"

The preacher exclaimed, "In the name of God! Why didn't you tell me the dog was a Baptist?"

DAI got a bit fed up with being teased by his relatives at weddings. Old aunts used to go up to him and say, "You're next!" They stopped after he started doing the same thing to them at funerals.

As was the custom in Sunday School, every child was expected to learn and recite a verse from the Bible. Poor Dewi never learnt any, so one Sunday, the preacher decided to help him for the next Sunday school.

"All you've got to say is, 'The Father, the Son and the Holy Ghost.'"

Dewi repeated this a few times, and the preacher thought for a few minutes, and pointed to the three buttons on his jacket, and said, "There we are – this will help you." He pointed to the top button, and said, "The Father," then the middle button, and said, "The Son," and, finally, to the bottom button, saying "The Holy Ghost."

The following Sunday, Dewi stood, and proudly said, "The Father, the Son, and sorry, sir, but my mother has sewn the Holy Ghost on my fly."

YOUNG Geraint was visiting the Chapel for the first time, checking all the announcements and posters along the walls. He came to a group of pictures of men in uniform.

He asked a nearby deacon, "Who are all those men in the pictures?"

The Deacon replied, "Why, those are village boys who died in the Service."

Dumbfounded, Geraint asked, "Was that the morning service or the evening service?"

CERI was one of the first to leave the church one day, and the preacher was standing at the door as usual, to shake hands. He grabbed Ceri by the hand and pulled him aside, saying, "You need to join the Army of the Lord!"

Ceri replied, "I'm already in the Army of the Lord, Mr Jones."

The preacher questioned, "How come I don't see you except at Christmas and Easter?"

He whispered back, "I'm in the secret service."

LITTLE Bethan was in chapel with her grandmother when she started feeling ill.

"Nain," she said, "can we leave now?"

"No," her grandmother replied.

"Well, I think I'm going to be sick!"

"Go out the front door, my little cariad, then around to the back of the chapel, and be sick behind the shed."

In about two minutes, Bethan returned to her seat.

"Were you sick?" her grandmother asked.

"Yes," Bethan replied.

"Well, you were very quick, going all the way to the back of the chapel and back so soon! "

"I didn't have to go out of the church, Nain," Bethan replied. "They have a box next to the front door that says 'for the sick.'"

THE new preacher wanted some holy water, so he filled a pan from the tap, and boiled the hell out of it.

The Welsh Salesman

WIL had the reputation of being a fantastic salesman. One day he visited a large department store in Cardiff and informed the manager:

"This computer will cut your workload by 50%.

The manager replied: "That's great, I'll take two."

WHAT flavour ice cream do you have?" Glyn asked the waitress.

"Strawberry, vanilla and chocolate," answered the new waitress, in a hoarse whisper. Trying to be sympathetic, Dai asked, "Do you have laryngitis?"

"No..." replied the new waitress with some effort, "just... er... vanilla, strawberry, and chocolate."

EMRYS started his job as a door-to-door vacuum cleaner salesman and managed to bull his way into a woman's home in the valleys.

"This machine is the best ever," he exclaimed, pouring a bag of dirt over the lounge floor. The woman says she's really worried it may not all come off, so Emrys says,

"If this machine doesn't remove all the dust completely, I'll lick it off myself."

"Do you want ketchup on it?" she says. "We're not connected for electricity yet!"

GRIFF was demonstrating unbreakable combs in a David Evans store. He was impressing onlookers by subjecting the comb to all kinds of torture and stress. Finally, to impress even the sceptics in the crowd, Griff bent the comb completely in half, and it snapped with a loud crack. Without missing a beat, he confidently held up both halves of the 'unbreakable' comb for everyone to see, and said,

"And this, ladies and gentlemen, is what an unbreakable comb looks like on the inside."

WATCYN started a job as a sales assistant at a large department store in south Wales. On his first day, the boss took him around to show him the ropes. As they were passing the gardening section, they heard a customer asking Wil, another sales assistant, for some grass seed. Wil then asked him:

"Excuse me, but will you be needing a hose to water your lawn?"

"That's a good idea. I hadn't thought of that. Yes, I'll take one," replied the customer.

"And how about some fertiliser and weed-killer?"

"Yes, good idea."

"Here's a couple of bags. You'll also need a lawn mower to cut the grass when it starts growing too long," said Wil.

"I'll take one of those, too," said the customer, before paying and leaving with his purchases. After the customer had left, the sales manager turned to Watcyn.

"See?" he said, "that's the way to make a good sale. Always sell more than the customer originally came in for."

Impressed, Watcyn went to the pharmaceutical section, where he was to work. Soon, a man strolled in and said, "I'd like some tampons, please."

Watcyn replied, "Certainly sir, and would you like a lawn mower, too?"

"What for?" said the customer.

"Well, you're not going to be doing much this weekend, sir, so you might as well mow the lawn."

A nun is undressing for a bath and while she's standing naked, there's a knock at the door.

The nun calls, "Who is it?"

A voice answers, "Ianto, a blind salesman."

The nun decides to allow herself a little thrill by letting Ianto into the bathroom while she's naked, so she lets him in.

Ianto walks in, clocks the nun, and says, "Bloody hell! Well, hello there, can I sell you a blind, cariad…?"

THREE girls from Swansea apply for a job, and are told that they will need to answer a question, and explain their answer. Blodwen goes first and is shown a cauliflower, a potato and a knife, and is asked which is the odd one out, and why. She thinks for a while and answers, "The knife," qualifying her answer with the explanation that the knife is long, while the other two are sort of round. This answer was accepted.

Next goes Myfanwy, who also chooses the knife; however, her explanation was that the knife was mineral, whilst the other objects were vegetable.

Mari fach is asked the same question, and after pondering for a few minutes, she answered, "The cauliflower. You can make chips with the other two!"

The Welsh during the War

D AI, Evan and Twm were taken prisoners in the jungle, and were just about to be executed in front of a firing squad.

"Follow my example," says Dai to the other two, and as the executing officer prepared to shoot him, he shouted, "Flash flood!" In the ensuing panic, Dai escaped into the jungle.

"That's a good idea," thought Evan, and as the squad were getting ready to shoot, Evan shouted, "Earthquake!" There was a major panic, during which Evan escaped into the jungle.

Twm thought to himself, "That's a good idea," and similarly, when the squad got themselves ready to shoot, Twm shouted "Fire!"

R OURKE'S Drift. The Welsh boys are under attack from the Zulus. Dai is right in the middle, giving them a rendering of '*We'll Keep a Welcome*'. Twenty Welsh boys go down during the Zulu charge. They regroup and charge again. This time, Dai gives them a bit of '*Sospan Fach*'. Another twenty Welsh lads go down. The Zulus regroup and charge again. Dai's singing '*Men of Harlech.*'

The sergeant major, under a hail of spears, shouts, "For God's sake, Dai, sing them something they bloody know!"

D URING World War II, Dai and Wil got lost in the Sahara desert. Realising their only chance of survival was to find civilisation, they began walking. After some time, they both became thirsty. More time passed, and soon they both began feeling faint. They were on the verge of passing out when they spied a tent about 500 metres in front of them. Barely conscious, they both reached the tent and called out, "Water!"

A Bedouin appeared at the entrance to the tent, and addressed them sympathetically, "I am sorry, sirs, I have no water. However, would you like to buy a tie?" With this, he brandished a collection of exquisite silken neckwear.

"You fool, we're both dying of thirst, and need water!"

"Well, sirs," replied the Bedouin, "If you really need water, there is a tent about two kilometres south of here where you can get some."

Without knowing how, Dai summoned sufficient strength to drag Wil all the way to the second tent. With his last ounce of strength, he pulled at the entrance to the tent and collapsed. Another Bedouin, dressed in a expensive tuxedo, appeared at the door and enquired, "Can I help you both?"

"Water..." was the feeble reply.

"Oh, dear," said the Bedouin, "I'm sorry, but you can't come in here without a tie!"

IT was during World War II, and Ifan and Dai were dismantling the bloodhound missile, at St Athans RAF base, when Dai noticed some fluid leaking from it. He touched it with his finger, smelt it, tasted it, and said, "Hey, Ifan! Taste this stuff."

It was bloody gorgeous, so they spent the first part of the afternoon dipping their fingers into the liquid and sipping it. This developed into a cup job, whereby they both filled their thermos cups with the liquid and supped away contentedly for the rest of the day.

The following morning, Dai had a tremendous hangover and decided to telephone Ifan.

"How are you this morning, Ifan?"

"I feel bloody awful," he replied, "but I'm glad I took a Thermos full of that stuff home."

"Aye," said Dai, "but for God's sake, don't fart – I'm phoning you from Tokyo!"

THE RSM of the Welsh Guards went out, only to find that none of his squaddies were there.

One finally ran up, panting heavily.

"Sorry, RSM! I can explain. You see, I had a date and it ran a little late. I ran to the bus, but missed it, then hitched a taxi, but it broke down. I found a farmhouse and borrowed a horse, but it dropped dead, so I ran 10 miles, and now I'm here."

The RSM was very sceptical about this explanation, but at least the man was here, so he let the squaddie go. Moments later, eight more squaddies came up to the RSM panting, and he asked them all why they were late.

"Sorry, boss! You see, I had a date and it ran a little late. I ran to the bus but missed it, then hitched a taxi, but it broke down. I found a farmhouse and borrowed a horse, but it dropped dead, so I ran 10 miles, and now I'm here."

The RSM eyed them, again feeling very sceptical, but since he'd let the first off lightly, he let them off as well. A ninth squaddie jogged up to the RSM, panting heavily.

"Sorry, boss! I had a date and it ran a little late. I ran to the bus but missed it, stopped a taxi, but..."

"Let me guess," interrupted the RSM, "it broke down."

"No," said the squaddie, "there were so many dead horses in the road, it took forever to get around them."

It was a dark, stormy night. The Welsh Guardsman was on his first assignment, which was guard duty. A general stepped out, taking his dog for a walk. The nervous young guardsman snapped to attention, made a perfect salute, and snapped out, "Sir, good evening, sir!"

The general, out for some relaxation, returned the salute, and said, "Good evening, guard. Nice night, isn't it?"

Well, in fact, it wasn't a nice night, but the guardsman wasn't going to disagree with the general, so the he saluted again, and replied, "Sir, yes sir!"

The general continued, "You know, there's something about a stormy night that I find soothing, it's really relaxing. Don't you agree?"

The guardsman didn't agree, but then he was just a private, and responded, "Sir, yes sir!"

The General, pointing at the dog, said, "this is a Golden Retriever, the best type of dog to train."

The Guardsman glanced at the dog, saluted yet again, and said, "Sir, yes sir!"

The General continued, "I got this dog for my wife."

The Guardsman said simply, "Good swap, sir!"

A British general had sent some of the Welsh Fusiliers off to fight for their country in the Falkland Islands crisis. Upon returning to England from the South American islands, three soldiers that had distinguished themselves in battle were summoned to the general's office.

"Since we weren't actually at war," the general began, "I can't award any medals. We did, however, want to let each of you know your efforts were appreciated. What we've decided to do is to let each of you choose two points on your body. You will be given £5 sterling for each inch of distance between those parts. We'll start on the left, boys, so what'll it be?"

"The tip of me head to me toes, sah!" said Dai.

"Very good, boy; that's 70 inches, which comes to £350," replied the general.

Ianto says, "The tip of the finger on one outstretched hand to the tip of the other, sir!"

"Even better, son. That's 72 inches, which comes to £360. And what about you, Evan?"

"The palm of me hand to the tip of me left gooly, sah!"

"A strange request, boy, but fair. Let's measure that." As the general starts to measure, he finds he cannot locate a certain part of Evan's anatomy.

"Hey boy, where is your left gooly?"

"On Goose Green, Sir!" replied Ianto.

Private Jones was brought up before the unit CO for returning late to barracks.

"You can take your choice, private – one month's restriction or twenty days' pay," said the officer.

"All right, sir," said Jones, "I'll take the money."

The Welsh away from Home

75

ISLWYN, Iwan and Morris were on their way to jail. They were allowed to take one item each with them, to help occupy their time while imprisoned.

In the Black Maria, Islwyn turned to the others and said, "So, what did you bring?"

Iwan answered, "A box of paints," and said that he intended to paint anything he could. He wanted to become the 'Kyffin Williams of the prison.'

Then Islwyn asked Morris, "What did you bring?"

Morris pulled out a deck of cards and said, "I brought cards. I can play poker, Chinese patience and snap, and any number of games."

Islwyn was grinning to himself. The other two noticed this and asked, "What are you so proud of? What did you bring?"

Islwyn pulled out a box of tampons and smiled. He said, "These."

"What good are those?" asked the other two, puzzled.

Dai grinned, and pointed to the box. "Well, according to this, I can go horseback riding, swimming, roller-skating..."

TWO old dears from the valleys arrived at Cardiff Airport and were asked.

"Did you have a nice trip?"

"We did, but we had to keep our seat belts on all the way because of the flatulence."

A beautiful young blonde from across the border boards a plane to New York – co-piloted by Jeremiah from Treorchy – with a ticket for standard accommodation. She looks at the standard seats, then looks into the first-class cabin. Seeing that the first-class seats appear to be much larger and more comfortable, she moves forward to the last empty one. The flight attendant checks her ticket and tells the woman that her seat is in standard.

"I'm young, blonde and beautiful, and I'm going to sit here all the way to New York," said the blonde.

Flustered, the flight attendant goes to the cockpit and informs the captain of the blonde problem. The captain goes back and tells the woman that her assigned seat is in standard.

Again, the blonde replies, "I'm young, blonde and beautiful, and I'm going to sit here all the way to New York."

The captain doesn't want to cause a scene, and so returns to the cockpit to discuss the blonde problem with Jeremiah. Jeremiah says that he has a blonde girlfriend, and that he can take care of the problem. He then goes back, and briefly whispers something in the blonde's ear.

She immediately gets up, says, "Thank you so much," hugs Jeremiah, and rushes back to her seat in the standard accommodation. The pilot and flight attendant, who were watching in rapt attention, ask Jeremiah what he had said to the woman.

He replied, "I just told her that the first-class section isn't going to New York."

IANTO wins a holiday to the Wild West, in the USA, during which he visits the local bar. Sitting all alone in the corner is an Indian, looking very old and decrepit.

"Who's that old geezer?" asks Ianto.

"That," says the barman, "is an old Indian medicine man. A font of all knowledge, he knows the answer to all questions."

Ianto, really impressed, wanders up to the old guy who greets him with, "How," as old American Indians are wont to do.

"*Shw mae*," says our Ianto, and asks him who Liverpool played in the 1986 FA cup final.

"Everton," replies the old man.

"What was the score?"

"3-1," replies the old guy.

"Amazing" says Ianto. "Now who scored the winner?"

"Souness, in the 82nd minute," replies the old man.

Now this has impressed the hell out of Ianto, who can't wait to get back to Wales, to tell all his butties about this old medicine man who knows everything, in the saloon bar out west.

Several years pass and Ianto finds himself back in that part of the USA. Remembering the old Indian, he goes back to the bar, just on the off-chance he's still alive. And there he is, still sitting in the same old corner, sipping root beer.

"How," says our Ianto, trying to impress with his colloquial Indian.

"Diving header from just outside the six yard box," replies the old Indian.

IANTO is in a bar, bragging AGAIN to the barman, that he knows everybody in the whole world.

The bartender, fed up with Ianto's bragging, says, "Okay, I bet you £100 that I can find three people you DO NOT know."

So Ianto says, "That's impossible, but go for it."

The next day, Ianto and the barman board a plane for Hollywood, and end up at Brad Pitt's door. They knock. Brad comes to the door, sees Ianto and says, "How the hell have you been, Ianto? It's been a long time!"

The barman is surprised, but says, "OK, I have two more people I know you don't know."

So after another plane trip, they end up in Washington DC at the White House. They knock on the door and Bush answers, sees Ianto, shakes his hand, and says, "Great to see you again, Ianto."

The barman is very surprised now, but has one more chance,

so to the Vatican they go. When they arrive, there are masses of people in the square waiting for the Pope to give his message. The bartender looks around and cannot find Ianto, smiles and says to himself, "I knew I could find someone Ianto didn't know. HA!" Then suddenly the Pope appears on his balcony, with Ianto by his side. Ianto looks down and sees the barman is passed out among the crowd, so he rushes down to see if he's all right.

He revives him and says, "What happened? Are you okay?"

The bartender says, "I was fine until the guy next to me asked me, 'Who's that guy up there with Ianto?' Here's your £100!"

DAI emigrates from the valleys to America. His first stop when he arrives in New York is at a bar in a funky section of the city. He orders a drink and spies beautiful women sitting a few stools away. He moves over to the young women, and, in his best English, he says, "My name Dai, from the valleys. You very beautiful. Can I buy a drink?"

The woman replies, "You're wasting your time and your money – I am a lesbian."

Dai is puzzled. "What is a lesbian?" he asks.

The woman replies, "I'll show you, honey."

At that point the woman walks down to the end of the bar, where another beautiful woman is sitting. The lesbian initiates some small talk and then gives the other woman a big, deep mouth kiss. The lesbian returns to her seat next to an astonished Dai. She says, "Now do you understand?"

Dai says, "Oh, yes – I am a lesbian, too!"

GOMER is on holiday in Cyprus, travelling with a courier through one of the remotest areas in the Troodos mountains, when they comes across an ancient temple. Gomer is intrigued by the temple, and asks the courier for details. The courier states that archaeologists are carrying out excavations, and still finding great treasures. Gomer then queries how old the temple is.

"This temple is 3503 years old," replies the courier.

Gomer, really impressed at this accurate dating, asks how he can give this precise figure.

"Easy," replies the courier. "The archaeologists said the temple was 3500 years old, and that was three years ago."

Other Welsh Jokes

THE Prince of Wales went to Merthyr Tydfil to open a supermarket. Throughout the ceremony he was wearing a hat made from fox fur. Everybody thought it a little strange, but said nothing, as he was the Prince, and thinking that it may have been an ancient ceremonial garment. After the supermarket was opened, the mayor thanked the prince, and commented upon his choice of headgear. The prince said that it had been his mother's idea.

"As I was leaving this morning, I told my mother I was going to Merthyr Tydfil, and she said, 'Merthyr Tydfil? Wear the fox hat.'"

IANTO was walking along Penarth beach and found a bottle. When he rubbed it, lo and behold, a genie appeared.

"I will grant you three wishes," announced the genie. "But, since Satan still hates me, for every wish you make, your rival, Brinley, gets the wish as well, but he gets double whatever you ask for."

Ianto thought about this for a while.

"For my first wish, I would like £10 million quid," he announced. Instantly, the genie gave him a Swiss bank account number and assured the man that £10 million had been deposited.

"But Brynley has just received £20 million," the genie said.

"I've always wanted a Ferrari," Ianto said. Instantly a Ferrari appeared.

"But Brynley has just received two Ferraris," the genie said. "And what is your last wish?"

"Well," said Ianto, "I've always wanted to donate a kidney for transplanting."

ONE day, Dafydd's mother was cleaning his room. In the wardrobe, she found an S&M bondage magazine. This was highly upsetting to her. She hid the magazine until his father got home. When Dafydd's father walked in the door, she irately handed the magazine to him, and said, "This is what I found in your son's wardrobe."

He looked at it and handed it back to her without a word. Several minutes passed, then she finally asked him, "Well, what should we do about this?"

He looked at her and said, "I don't think you should spank him."

AN Audi Quattro with five Irishmen in it was pulled up at the customs office at Fishguard Harbour. Evan, the customs officer, said to them, "You are entering Wales illegally. 'Quattro' means four, and there are five of you."

One of the Irishmen replied that Quattro was the name of the car and had nothing to do with the number of passengers.

Evan replied, "You can't pull the wool over my eyes with that story. I'm afraid I'm going to have to arrest you all."

"We demand to see your supervisor," said the driver. "That was an idiotic statement."

"Can't," said Evan. "He's arresting two people in a Fiat Uno!"

GWYNETH, a flight attendant at Cardiff Wales airport, was stationed at the departure gate to check tickets. As a man approached, she extended her hand for the ticket, and he opened his trench coat and flashed her. Without missing a beat she said, "Sir, I asked to see your ticket, not your stub."

GERAINT was a successful lawyer, but as he got older he was increasingly hampered by incredible headaches. When his career and love life started to suffer, he sought medical help. After being referred from one specialist to another, he finally came across an old country doctor who solved the problem.

"The good news is that I can cure your headaches. The bad news is that it will require castration. You have a very rare condition which causes your testicles to press up against the base of your spine and the pressure creates one hell of a headache. The only way to relieve the pressure is to remove the testicles."

Geraint was shocked and depressed. Wondering if he had anything to live for, he couldn't concentrate long enough to answer, but decided he had no choice but to go under the knife. When he left the hospital, he was without a headache for the first time in 20 years. Nevertheless, he felt he was missing an important part of himself, but as he walked down the street, he realised that he felt like a different person. He could make a new beginning and live a new life.

He saw a men's clothing store and thought, "That's what I need, a new suit."

He entered the shop and told the salesman, "I'd like a new suit."

The elderly tailor eyed him briefly and said, "Let's see... size 44. Long."

Geraint laughed, and said, "That's right! How did you know?"

"Been in the business 60 years."

Geraint tried on the suit. It fitted perfectly. As he admired himself in the mirror, the salesman asked, "How about a new shirt?"

Geraint thought for a moment then said, "Sure."

The salesman eyed Geraint and said, "Let's see... 34 sleeve, and... 16 ½ neck." Geraint was surprised, "That's right! How did you know?"

"Been in the business 60 years."

Geraint tried on the shirt, and it fitted perfectly. As he adjusted the collar in the mirror, the salesman asked, "How about new shoes?"

Geraint was on a roll and said, "Sure."

The salesman eyed Geraint's feet and said, "Let's see. 9 ½ E."

Geraint was astonished. "That's right! How did you know?"

"Been in the business 60 years."

Geraint tried on the shoes and they fitted perfectly. He walked comfortably around the shop and the salesman asked, "How about some new underwear?"

Geraint thought for a second and said, "Sure."

The salesman stepped back, eyed his waist and said, "Let's see... size 36."

Geraint laughed and said, "Aha! Got you! I've worn size 34 since I was 18 years old."

The salesman shook his head. "You can't wear a size 34. It will press your testicles up against the base of your spine and give you one hell of a headache."

WIL turned to Ianto at the end of the shift and asked him if he'd mind letting Mari, his wife, know that he'd been asked to work the next shift.

"Not at all," replied Ianto.

On his way home, he called at Wil's to pass the message on to Mari, and after his cup of tea with Mari, they started reminiscing about the old days.

"Jiw," he said, "Mari, you always had a nice pair of breasts. I'll give you £20 if you show them to me, just for old times' sake."

"Jiw, jiw, no," said Mari, "I'm happily married to Wil now.

I couldn't do that, but, on the other hand, if Wil didn't know about it, well, I suppose the money would come in useful."

After she had obliged, they both got a bit excited, and Ianto said,

"Tell you what, Mari, I'll give you another £20 if you just let me touch them. Wil will never get to find out."

"Oh, Ianto, you are a one! Just this once, then, but not a word to Will."

After she had obliged, Ianto couldn't resist the temptation, and said, "Mari, I'll give you another £30 to see you in your birthday suit."

Mari said, "Well, only because the money will come in useful, and not a word to Wil."

Ianto couldn't resist it, and said, "Mari, just for old times' sake, I'll give you all I've got left – £63.76 – if you'll go to bed with me."

Well, after humming and ha-ing, she thought the money would come in useful, and they went to bed for the rest of the afternoon. That night, Wil came home, tired after a hard day's work.

"Did Ianto call and tell you that I was working a doubler, Mari?"

"Why, yes," she replied.

"And did he give you my wages, £133.76?"

D AI ran out of the hospital in his birthday suit, screaming blue murder, and staff nurse Myfanwy Jones followed him, with a kettle in her hand. The surgeon shouted,

"No, nurse, I told you to prick his boil!"

MYFANWY goes down her local and orders drinks for all. After serving everyone, the barman asked her, "What's the occasion?"

Myfanwy answers, "Well, Dai and me just finished a 300-piece jigsaw puzzle in just one month!"

The barman asked as delicately as possible, "One month, huh? Don't you think that a little long for a 300-piece puzzle?"

"Of course not," said Myfanwy. "It said on the box 2-4 years!"

DAI, a bricklayer from Bangor, had filled in an accident report form...

"Dear Sir, I am writing in response to your request for additional information on the accident report form I submitted as to the cause of my accident. You require a fuller explanation and I trust the following details will be sufficient.

"I am a bricklayer by trade. On the day of the accident, I was working alone on the roof of a new six-storey building in Caernarfon. When I completed my work, I found I had some bricks left over, which, when weighed later were found to be slightly in excess of two hundredweight, i.e. over 224 lbs. Rather than carry the bricks down by hand, I decided to lower them in a barrel, by using a pulley, which was attached to the side of the building, on the eighth floor. Securing the rope at ground level, I went up to the roof, swung the barrel out and loaded the bricks into it. Then I went down and untied the rope, holding it tightly to ensure a slow descent of the bricks.

"You will note in Block 11 of the accident report form that I weigh 135 lbs. Due to my surprise at being jerked off the ground so suddenly, I lost my presence of mind and forgot to let go of the rope. Needless to say, I proceeded at a rapid rate up the side of the building. In the vicinity of the fourth floor, I met the barrel, which was now proceeding downward at an equally impressive speed. This explains the fractured skull, minor abrasions and the broken collarbone, as listed in the accident report form.

"Slowed only slightly, I continued my rapid ascent, not stopping until the fingers of my right hand were two knuckles deep into the pulley. Fortunately, by this time, I had regained my presence of mind and was able to hold tightly to the rope, in spite of the excruciating pain I was now beginning to experience. At approximately the same time, however, the barrel of bricks hit the ground, and the bottom fell out of the barrel. Now devoid of the weight of the bricks, that barrel weighed approximately half a hundredweight, i.e. some 56 lbs. I refer you again to my weight.

"As you might imagine, I began a rapid descent, down the side of the building. In the vicinity of the fourth floor, I again met the barrel; this time it was coming up. This accounts for the two fractured ankles, broken tooth and severe lacerations of my legs and lower body. Here my luck began to change slightly. The encounter with the barrel seemed to slow me enough to lessen my injuries when I fell into the pile of bricks and, fortunately, only three vertebrae were cracked. I am sorry to report, however, that as I lay there on the pile of bricks, in pain, unable to move, I again lost my composure and presence of mind and let go of the rope, and I lay there watching the empty barrel begin its journey back down onto me. This explains the two broken legs. I trust that this information will suffice."

A young punk gets on the number 26 bus in Cardiff. He has spiked, multi-coloured hair that's green, purple and orange. His clothes are a tattered mix of leather rags. His legs are bare, and he's wearing worn-out shoes. His entire face and body are riddled with pierced jewellery and his earrings are big, bright feathers. He sits down in the only vacant seat, directly across from Dickie, who glares at him for the next ten miles.

Finally, the punk gets self-conscious and barks at Dickie, "What are you looking at, you old fart? Didn't you ever do anything wild when you were young?"

Without missing a beat, Dickie replies: "Yeah, back when I was young and in the Navy, I got really drunk one night in Singapore and made love to a parrot... I was just wondering if you were my son."

DAI is taking his Rottweiler out for a walk. It is a hot day and, after a while, he decides to call in the Bull for a pint. The barman tells him dogs are not allowed, and he must tie it up outside. A few pints later, a woman walks into the bar and asks if someone has a large dog out front.

Dai proudly pipes up, "Yes, it's my Rottweiler; why do you ask?"

"It's dead," she blurts out.

"Did you hit it with your car?" asks Dai, stunned.

"No, my dog killed it," she replies.

Knowing how powerful a dog the Rottweiler is, he poses the question to her, "Pit-bull?"

"No, I have a Chihuahua," comes the answer.

Puzzled, he asks, "How did your Chihuahua kill my Rottweiler?"

"Well, I'm no vet," she replies, "but I think she got stuck in his throat."

TWO penguins walk into a bar. A third penguin says, "You'd have thought the second one would have seen it."

A blonde with a pig walks into the Queen's. The barman looks them up and down and says, "Where did you get that dumb animal?"

The pig replies, "I won her in a raffle."

THE police received a telephone call from number 57 complaining that a cat had broken into the house.

"If it's a cat," said the officer, "there's nothing to worry about. Who's that calling?"

"The parrot," was the reply.

A goldfish walks into a bar, jumps up on a bar stool, and looks at the barman really hard.

And the barman asks the goldfish, "What can I get you?"

Goldfish keeps looking at the guy, really deep and hard, and gasps: "Water."

DAI and Wil are in a bar having a couple of pints.

Dai says, "My mother-in-law's an angel."

Wil replies, "You're lucky! Mine's still alive!"

WHILST visiting the Pontardulais Agricultural Show, Jack Tŷ Mawr visited the Fortune-teller, and bought a crystal ball as a present for his wife.

"How much did this cost you?" enquired his wife when he got home.

"Good, isn't it?" said Jack, "and it was only £25."

"Good gosh!" said his wife. "They must have seen you coming."

IANTO Evans from Llandeilo proudly walked into the fishmonger's with rather a large sewin under his arm.

"Do you make fish cakes?" he proudly asked the fishmonger.

"As a matter of fact we do," replied the fishmonger.

"Good," said Ianto. "Can you make him one for his birthday tomorrow?"

DAI, Ianto and Wil work for the same computer firm, and are, respectively, a software manager, a hardware manager, and a marketing manager. They are driving to a meeting together when they have a puncture. They all get out of the car and look at the problem. Dai, the software manager, says, "I can't do anything about this - it's a hardware problem."

Ianto, the hardware manager, says, "Maybe, if we turned the car's engine off and on again, it would fix itself."

Wil, the marketing manager says, "75% of it is working – let's flog it!"

THREE cafés have all been in business for years, on the same block in Llanelli. After years of peaceful co-existence, Joe's café decides to put a sign in the window saying: 'We make the best coffee in Llanelli.'

Wil's café soon followed suit, and put a sign in their window proclaiming: 'We make the best coffee in the world.'

Finally, Dai's caff put a sign up, saying: 'We make the best coffee on the block.'

ALUN is playing a round of golf by himself and is about to tee off, when a salesman runs up to him and yells, "Wait! Before you tee off, I have something really amazing to show you!"

Alun, rather perturbed, says, "What is it?"

"It's a special golf ball," says the salesman. "You can never lose it!"

"What do you mean," said Alun, "you can never lose it? What if you hit it into the sea off the second?"

"No problem," says the salesman. "It floats, and it detects where the beach is, and spins towards it."

"Well, what if you hit it onto the road and out of bounds?"

"Easy," says the salesman. "It detects the boundary, and rolls back in within two clubs lengths."

"Well, what if you hit into the deep rough?" asks Alun.

"It emits a beeping sound, and you can find it with your eyes closed."

"Okay," says Alun, really impressed. "But what if your round goes late and it gets dark?"

"No problem, sir, this golf ball glows in the dark! I'm telling you, you can never lose this golf ball!" Alun buys it at once.

"Just one question," he says to the salesman. "Where did you get it?"

"I found it."

A secretary was leaving the office, one Friday evening, when she met Hywel, the Human Resources Manager, standing in front of a shredder with a piece of paper in his hand.

"Listen," said Hywel, "this is important, and my secretary has already left. Can you make this thing work?"

"Certainly," said the secretary. She turned the machine on, inserted the paper, and pressed the start button.

"Excellent, excellent!" said Hywel, as his paper disappeared inside the machine. "I just need one copy."

GORONWY was given the job of painting the white lines down the middle of a road. On his first day, he painted six miles; the next day, three miles; the following day, less than a mile. When the boss asked Goronwy why he kept painting less each day, he replied, "I just can't do any better. Each day, I keep getting farther away from the paint can."

A preacher dies and, when he gets to heaven, he sees a Cardiff taxi driver who has more crowns. He says to an angel, "I don't get it. I devoted my whole life to my congregation."

The angel says, "We reward results. Did your congregation always pay attention when you gave a sermon?"

The preacher says, "Once in a while, someone fell asleep."

The angel says, "Right. And when people rode in this fellow's taxi, they not only stayed awake, but they usually prayed!"

IAN is hired by the circus to perform a necessary but rather unpleasant task. His job is to walk behind the elephants in the ring, shovelling their droppings as they walk about. After a rather tiring evening at work, he goes to the circus bar, sits with other workers, and begins complaining about his work.

"It's just terrible, walking behind those huge animals, first dodging, then shovelling aside the shit. My arms are tired, my shoes and pants are a mess, and I'll have to shower before I return home, because of the stink."

His butties agree: "Why don't you just quit the job and find something better. You must have some skills and talents that you can put to use somewhere else."

Ian looks at them in amazement: "You know, you could be right, but I just can't give up the glamour of show business!"

THE Railway Inspector asked Evan, "What would you do if you realised that two trains were heading for each other on the same track?"

Evan answers, "I'd switch the points for one of the trains."

"What if the lever broke?" asked the inspector.

"Well, then I'd dash down out of the signal box," said Evan, "and I'd use the manual lever over there."

"What if that had been struck by lightning?"

"Then," Evan answers, "I'd run back into the signal box and phone the next signal box."

"What if the phone was engaged?"

"Well, in that case," persevered Evan, "I'd rush down out of the box and use the public emergency phone at the level crossing up there."

"What if that was vandalised?"

"Oh, well, then I'd run into the village and get my uncle Tom."

This puzzles the inspector, so he asks, "Why would you do that?"

Came the answer, "My Uncle Tom has never seen a train crash."

DAI was sitting on Constitution Hill in Aberystwyth, watching the world go by, when a visitor asked him how far you could see on a clear day.

"You can see further than America," said Dai.

"What a load of nonsense," said the visitor.

"You can, honestly," said Dai. "You can see the moon!"

DAI, Evan and Ianto are in the school yard, bragging how great their fathers are. Dai says,

"My father's the fastest runner. He can fire an arrow, and then run to the target before the arrow."

Evan says, "Bull. You think that's fast! My father can shoot his gun and be there before the bullet."

Ianto listens in amazement and shakes his head. He then says, "That's nothing. My father works for the council. He stops working at 4:30 and he is home by 3:45!"

A doctor, a lawyer and a manager were discussing the relative merits of having a wife or a mistress.

The lawyer says, "For sure, a mistress is better. If you have a wife and want a divorce, it causes all sorts of legal problems."

The doctor says, "It's better to have a wife because the sense of security lowers your stress and is good for your health."

The manager says, "You're both wrong. It's best to have both, so that when the wife thinks you're with the mistress, and the mistress thinks you're with your wife – you can go to the office and do some work."

D AI telephones his solicitor's office and says, "I want to speak to my solicitor."

The receptionist replies, "I'm sorry, but he died last week

The next day, Dai phones again and asks the same question.

The receptionist replies, "I told you yesterday, he died last week."

The next day, Dai calls again and asks to speak to his solicitor.

By this time the receptionist is getting a little annoyed and says, "I keep telling you that your solicitor died last week. Why do you keep calling?"

"Because I just love hearing it."

W IL and Gomer were in a restaurant and ordered fish. The waiter brought a dish with two fish, one larger than the other.

Gomer said to Wil, "Help yourself."

Wil helped himself to the larger fish.

After a tense silence, Gomer said, "Really, now, if you'd given me first choice, I would have taken the smaller fish!"

Wil replied, "What are you complaining for? You've got it, haven't you?"

DAI and Wil went into a café and ordered two teas. Then, they produced packed sandwiches from their pockets and started to eat. The waiter became quite concerned, marched over and told them, "You can't eat your own sandwiches in here!"

Dai and Wil looked at each other, shrugged their shoulders and then swapped sandwiches.

A penguin walks into a bar in Tenby; he goes to the counter and asks the barman, "Have you seen my brother?"

The barman asks, "What does he look like?"

FRED was asked, "With what would you connect William Hague?"

He replied, "With a hyphen."

TWM walked up to the station porter at Abercwmport and complained that the road to the station was too long. The Porter replied that if it were any shorter, it wouldn't reach the trains.